DATE DUE

MAR 2 1 2007			
GAYLORD			PRINTED IN U.S.A.

THE RETURN MESSAGE

THE BARNARD WOMEN POETS PRIZE

Edited by Saskia Hamilton

2003 *Figment* Rebecca Wolff
Chosen by Eavan Boland
and Claudia Rankine

2004 *The Return Message* Tessa Rumsey
Chosen by Jorie Graham

ALSO BY TESSA RUMSEY

Assembling the Shepherd

THE
RETURN MESSAGE

POEMS

Tessa Rumsey

W. W. NORTON & COMPANY

New York • London

For information about permission to reproduce selections from
this book, write to Permissions, W. W. Norton & Company, Inc.,
500 Fifth Avenue, New York, NY 10110

Manufacturing by The Courier Companies, Inc.
Book design by Charlotte Staub Thomas
Production manager: Amanda Morrison

Library of Congress Cataloging-in-Publication Data

Rumsey, Tessa, 1970–
The return message : poems / Tessa Rumsey.—1st ed.
p. cm.
ISBN 0-393-06051-9 (hardcover)
I. Title.
PS3568.U458R48 2005
811'.54—dc22
2005000937

W. W. Norton & Company, Inc.
500 Fifth Avenue, New York, N.Y. 10110
www.wwnorton.com

W. W. Norton & Company Ltd.
Castle House, 75/76 Wells Street, London W1T 3QT

1 2 3 4 5 6 7 8 9 0

ACKNOWLEDGMENTS

Special thanks to Pierre Jeanrenaud for thoughts and guidance regarding solar genesis, and to Jennifer Shulman, for lighting a dark path I thought I might never find.

Thanks to the editors of the following journals, print and online,
in which some of these poems first appeared:
*Boston Review, Conjunctions, Colorado Review, Electronic Poetry Review,
INTERIM, POOL, Ploughshares,* Slope.org, *Verse,* Verse.com.

For Michael

"Not every end is a goal. The end of a melody is not its goal; but nonetheless, if the melody had not reached its end it would not have reached its goal. A parable."

—Friedrich Nietzsche

"Another time I saw a child coming toward me holding a lighted torch in his hand. 'Where have you brought the light from?' I asked him. He immediately blew it out, and said to me, 'O Hasan, tell me where it is gone, and I will tell you whence I fetched it.'"

—Hasan Basri

CONTENTS

CONTENTS

THE RETURN MESSAGE

COUNTDOWN TO PEARL STRING OF PLANETS

Young foliage sweet bronze.
Most strongly scented of all wisterias.
Deep spring: overcome by my own perfume.

X

What if you—abandoned yourself? Dislocation, as in a time of great danger or impending

IX

Physical annihilation, the way the—soul?—may discover the liberty to disconnect

VIII

From the body, like the word *money* from the mint or an individual copper penny

VII

And what exactly does it mean to wonder about this over coffee, solitude, perfect

VI

Weather? They gather he shifted from side to side to prevent the road from dismantling

V

His skin as he was dragged on / down the highway. Unchained—as they say in revolutions

IV

And country music—for this? Reader, the luscious branches of the southern magnolia

III

Were lopped off and in the aftermath the tree simply—prospered. For what purpose

II

Was that man offered? What are the end of the world maps like—is there a general panic

I

That can be expressed spatially—tell me the driver didn't know where he was going—

Before you met me, growing wild on every hillside.
Scrambling in hedges by the footpath, hanging over.
Rocks, dipping leaves and flowers into the canals and mountain streams of No-Where.

APRIL FOOLS

Inside the pale niagara of her cruel betrayal: a paper boat, not.
Afloat; but not sinking into azure ether either—sailing.
The way a lost faith sails, limp and broken, but somewhere.
Still believing, it may be, you said to me, that we are not.
Yet built or sufficiently enlightened to do the thing we must.
Forgive her. Late winter: frozen cherries / atop a new parable.
Of my wicked stepmother. We are cherry blossoms caught.
Inside the static loop of loss. It's spring again—*She leaves us.*
You say the word again, *forgiveness*, holding your split heart.
In your hands, a frozen boat. Paper blossom. Olive branch.

JUNE INSIDE YOU

Luxurious lavender ticket.

To see the wisteria at Ushijima.

I once was a dwelling of young trees, fastened together with tough shoots, roof thatched with the grass called *kava*.

JUNE INSIDE YOU

Oh, how like a clock the lover lost its pale face and colored.

Numbers the longer you looked at it, until each phantom.

Tick of its innermost mechanism heralded possession.

And the mercurial sensation that something was slipping.

Away from you, until what once was your seduction device.

For measuring time had now become your myth: Abandonment.

To lead you, said the clock, said the lover, *we must leave you.*

And when there was no hope, when the wild horse watched you.

From the death field, you stood, frozen and alone, the black.

Willows ticking, *this is your failure*. Stop. *This is your blossoming.*

How should one view what has been conditioned?
(These flowers, hanging from my fingertips, no longer impress me.)
It's mythic, the desire to create what one once was content to become.

You are dying. To be conscious of this fact in the arms of the Beloved resembles the most beautiful trainwreck in the world, or religion. To be conscious of the hands' slow disintegration between waves of consumption and lovemaking is terror, to press one set of lips in time to another set of lips (in time) is both tragic and ignites the question of ambition, of the usefulness of kissing when seconds are slipping away from you. Napoleon sang this tune. Napoleon ordered his minions to plant twin dreams of elm trees in the future of the path he walked on, to ensure radiant grandeur and plutonic shade, to be *le plus grand chose* in the world while (paradoxically) feeling a coolness of shadows upon him. An unattainable dream is the lifeblood of being, like sap, like breathing. The mountain water rioting into the watershed was once on its way to the ether, much like you, *Ami*, once like you. Dying or fading or enrapt in tears of the Beloved, still conspiring toward the same plot, Voyager, still appearing as an instant of pain in the sudden flash of a blackbird's blood wing. Every spring we are haunted by a wave, a wave of red wings learning to fly low across the meadow, each flash of crimson unfolding from its dark envelope a love note inscribed with recollections of the Beloved, who left you long ago, who returns as a dream each spring, one which you cannot wake from. To be conscious of a recurring dream in which one defies the world of the waking and is reunited with the object of desire is shameful, to wake from a dream regretful is the ugliest sun in the world, is the body's hideous technology otherwise known as "a time machine." Once seen quietly blooming from an alleyway in the famous City of No-Name, a conspiracy of purple trees cannot be forgotten. In autumn, you walked down cobbled streets hungry for an unknown season, one resembling the Paradox of Cherry Blossoms, standing for winter and spring simultaneously, surprised by one yet stuck in the other—obsession, night sweats, terror. To be under the impression that spring is fueled by ambition is to declare free will the most powerful sun in the world, is to wrap fate up in thermonuclear plastic and bury it under a bank of toxic landfill. To hoard, to kill, to collect one trinket from each village taken under the guise of "ethnic clarification," to march, to bloom, to spring into action at the mention of revolution—to kiss a set of lips for the last time, Voyager, to choose one path at the expense of the other: obsession. Night sweats. Terror. At one edge of the empire, the handful of Himalayan Blue Poppies was a study in individuality, inside a wave, a wave of red and orange flowers architected within the royal garden's blood wing. In spring, you were never afraid inside that collective color; you felt protected; one

The Persistent Desire For Replica: To Rest Beneath a Pergola
Preserved by plants in full bloom, halcyon curtain of flowers. Each year.
Same scene: inhaling scent, listening to bees, the body still, deteriorating.

among many others; *a marching forest*; unconscious of dying; unconscious of ambition; *a crowd system*; until you met your inner Napoleon. To break free from a wave of crimson under the auric guise of ambition is the most promiscuous transaction in the world, or evolution. To cover a city in ultrasuede, to fall in love with Caesar, to walk beneath the purple flower's spring cathedral believing it, too, strives to shine brighter than any other on its path into ether—much like you, *Ami*, once like you. The dream was there to startle you, the season was there to wind you up like a trainwreck from whose tracks you must endlessly begin again—conspiring toward the same plot, Voyager, appearing as an instant of pain—now visible—upon the lost—the purple lips of the Beloved. Black wing. As always. It's spring.

Everything comes to pass exactly as it does—

An expedition was sent to observe and capture species in the wild.

Lost in endless spring, how else could we become one with the Beloved?

NEW WORLD CLOUD FOREST

The question attached to this colonial cage: could you, like Audubon, kill your subjects.

To study them? I adored you until I captured you, at which point the acquisition turned.

To loss, as you began to resemble what I had become most familiar with: a mirror.

A hairbrush, a feverish way of sipping tea in the morning and a languid way of taking tea.

In the afternoon, an abundance of writing implements, a shrinking vocabulary, light.

Shining from previously dark spaces. Electric wire. A machete. The desire to possess.

The sun, or perhaps one of the smaller planets twinkling like a fist against the indigo—

Emperor. History. Louis. Apollo. A clock on the mantle designed to move forward;

An imported cloud forest whose fate it was to *do no harm*, by which imperial timepiece.

Did you set your inner empire? Questions, like their keepers, blow back like bones.

To dust, and the rest of us: left wandering the wreckage of cages and their answers—

A parrot and its picture, the eye of the bird's last lover staring imprisoned from the page.

And if you ask how I . . . *found* the Beloved.

"The waves that came out of it, they were like surf waves."

Rolling in warm air. Suspended in spring. So many flowers. I could not breathe.

NOTES ON COINAGE

We begin to "think" the city into being; there is nothing to think; we wander hopelessly into believing.

The Beloved is *wallpaper*; the room in which you spend the night is *defined by unbearable architecture*.

Like an eclipse, a heartbeat disappears from its chest only when *overwhelmed* by a sound more sumptuous.

Than itself; this disparity points languidly to the genesis of wealth; and thus I came to be a pauper.

Inside your highly reflective city; whereas elsewhere I was rich enough to think (the Beloved into being).

How could I have known *Pharaoh asks from his throne* that something wasn't right here *while a profusion*.

Of symbols passes through Egypt like coinage, buying a harbinger here and a heretic there, portraying.

A swarm as innocuous as weather; so that later; amidst the spoils of empire; the conqueror can utter.

It was there all along (an incestuous song) or, more historically: *my loneliness is killing me—*

We are indebted—to every loss—for in its wake—it leaves us.

The half-broken battlements and outdated currency *conscripting the metropolis of memory*.

Our fortune's future rests (at best) upon our ability to interpret signs; as if losing one's *place* were losing.

One's *mind*; and where was I? Splendid as a child and shy, asking why, *why is there blood in the Nile?*

SPECIAL TRANSMISSION OUTSIDE THE TEACHING

Canterbury Bells, hyacinths.

Bluebells, African violets.

Each spring we dream of royal pigments, till one albino plant unveils a pink variant—

SPECIAL TRANSMISSION OUTSIDE THE TEACHING

Your life, like the river, could be seen from above as an operable topography, a study in entropy.

A *destabilizing navigation*, stumbling up the stairs with your addiction hat on, flowing around.

The city in a trance of almost unnoticeable anguish—I was your witness, and could see you.

When the cherry blossoms floated down like paper coins and the moon covered the entrance.

To the great void thin as rice paper; *what stands between myself and pain can be seen through.*

Clear as water. I watched you stare down the river. And pray for poverty when the money came.

Because to believe that a gift of Ming cloisonné or the baroque occurrence of springtime.

Belonged to you was terror, because you could not love the world enough to deny your desire.

To own it. There is, in spring, a euphoria that vines around the streets of this city like a pink.

And perfect sadness. You were its only witness. And because you insisted on watching it grow.

From a distance, you could not taste its sugary truth between your lips, nor could you possess it—

MORE IMPORTANT THAN THE DESIGN OF CITIES
WILL BE THE DESIGN OF THEIR DECAY

Where did you grow, before your roots took hold in the garden?
Curiouser and curiouser, this allegiance you seem to have with rocks.
Bluish blooms bathed in perfection, the moon shines fresh as you melt away.

MORE IMPORTANT THAN THE DESIGN OF CITIES
WILL BE THE DESIGN OF THEIR DECAY

Loneliness is a laboratory; its territory is forever defined; for reasons beyond our conviction

It cannot be lessened; only *redirected* and made to resemble *a crumbling heaven* or the year's

Grand delusion: *I shall no longer want for that which left me long ago*—go slow, said the soul,

That you may know the streets of your abandoned city more intimately than any joy

Or cherished season. We were in collusion, this city and I, creating a mythology of desolation;

Feeling utterly evacuated; yet methodically structured; in a post-Roman Empire; previously

Doomed sort of way—and what did the soul say, but *know it better*, then in a fever, *go deeper.*

There are days, I told the translator, when the veil drops and I am no longer inside the No-

Place most familiar, built by me long ago, and I walk through the world as if made real

By the existence of others and the casual way a crowd pauses together on a concrete curbside—

Perhaps one of them is weeping, perhaps another will gently reach out and twist a knife

Into my heart and we will lock eyes, and I will fall to my knees, and for a moment

He will hold me. What will I remember? The cold blade's cruel demeanor? My body

As it seizures? Or the gesture of my destroyer, showing me that in this life, I was not alone.

Tender leaves are sometimes eaten, often used in place of tea.

I bloomed so quickly no one could dissemble me.

No seeds baked in fire. No bark for rope and sandals. No branches for cables, or bridge making.

THE EXPANSION OF THE SELF

Does glass count as a wall?

Does a wall made of glass meet building codes determined in the South of France?

Does French glass reflect the pale light of springtime in the coastal village of Antibes, landscape of *plein air* and perpetual ennui, home of the author's first kiss and subsequent disfigurement—

Will local glass reflect Antibes more authentically than glass imported from another continent?

Will the world seen through a window appear *altered* depending upon where the glass within its frame was *manufactured?*

(Is the world seen through broken glass *whole* or is it *fractured?*)

The kiss had a desperate tone: "Dear so-and-so, you are my last chance—"

Later, unconscious by the side of the road: *is this fate?*

Or *is this circumstance?*

Will a lost world spend its last days pleading for survival?

Is there a name for *invisible cultural artifacts* suspended on a molecular level?

Does glass count as a wall?

The kiss was meant to be a masterpiece: "a mythological experience—"

In tune with Trojan horses: in tune with solar genesis.

The lyric theme of flourishing gardens—

Those things we most long for, buried in earth.

My invisible seed, my secret cool water, my cascading wisteria, my imminent birth.

Clockwork romeo spidering—along—the outside wall of a building—feeling for her window—the footing getting thin—

Satellite stalking the sun's circumference: satellite fearing the sun's hot rim.

Which came first: *beauty*?

Or *disfigurement*?

(First came consequence: next, the accident.)

If a speaker is uncertain, can a statement be a question?

Does a window reflecting occupants fulfill its *occupation*?

Contradiction Number One: we are bound by desire / *we are bound by the sun.*

Contradiction Number Two: my face in the glass / *the glass seen straight through.*

If each world stops at walls of its interior—

(Where one body begins, where the next body ends—)

Isn't a wall a way of *rubbing up against*, of *joining*, of *letting in*?

Because history is full of distance and endless revision, "the kiss" came to resemble a window on the Mediterranean—

A window, that when opened, granted a view of the world both *utterly changed* and *exactly the same*—

Antibes in endless revision: Antibes held in a picture frame.

(Contradiction Number Three: the only certainty / is the uncertainty of ennui)

How long have you felt it, this desire to move past spring?

Flowers die before their season.

Can I say "summer" and not disappear? In dreams I vanish, and am my own mirror.

It would be a summer night made famous by both its *harmony* and *antithesis*—

Her face pressed to his petulant lips: her face pressed to the pavement.

How does a person inhabit a house—

A *beautiful* house—

A house of *disfigurement*—

(A house perched precariously between *romantic* and *revisionist*)

A house now, a body now, seen through, like glass, opened as a window, the air rushing in, closed as an interior, the air wearing thin—

Wall of glass, roof of stone, to be *on display* yet *utterly alone*—

Coastal village, a foreign ennui, romeo at the window, fumbling for a key—

(Does glass count as a wall?)

First the accident: next the kiss: then the question:

Does the soul—exist?

As wilderness: attached to stems and branches of trees.

As ornament: trained through trelliswork, on arbors, over porticos, across a wooden bridge.

As a lamp: grown in a pot, symmetrical, in a dwarfed state, bending with pendulous blossoms, a floral fountain.

WILDERNESS IS EVERYWHERE

Do you have roots? Or do you *picture yourself* an astronaut inside a bubble suit.

Altitudinous above the troposphere, suspended *like candy* below the exosphere.

Connected to a stalled, mechanized version of your future self by a twisting.

Gold umbilicus: *how sweet* to be (simultaneously) the perpetrator *and* the crime's.

Sole witness: a mythical scenario, whose countless moving parts are played.

By the very hands that wind them! Oh, *listen*—this voice you hear, whether.

Your own, whispering the words *save me from myself*, or mine, is borrowed.

From a river, a babble that resembles "Stolen Water Rights in California."

Or *Fables of the Reconstruction*: there is a ribboned continuum: like *infinite* candy.

Forever streaming high above us: at times dipping down and filling our bodies.

With a sweetness too strange to mention, then leaving us alone to answer.

The echo of our questions—*did I create myself? This golden cord? My rescue mission?*

A TIME WHEN TRAINS MATTERED

Vigorous deciduous climber.

Twining anticlockwise.

Turning inward after your departure, I cannot comment on the leaves' color before falling.

A TIME WHEN TRAINS MATTERED

The dream where wilderness is beautiful *because* you are a part of it.

The dream where you cannot sleep, consumed by the very *thought* of it.

The dream when you said *wake me*, then *build me*, then *last forever*.

The dream of being left behind; the dream of moving faster.

The dream when your departure refigured the endless loop of landscape.

The dream devoid of heartache.

(The dream that never came.)

The dream where you return to feed me birthday cake, then fuck me.

The dream of mechanistic dream feedback; dream wandering.

The dream when the birth of trains became the sound of human suffering.

EVERLASTING GOBSTOPPER

I

In and around cool Beijing, wisterias fashioned to grow up trees.

Maximum pow in bamboo pergolas.

It *is* heartbreaking: growing over piled rocks.

EVERLASTING GOBSTOPPER

I

You may ask yourself / you may tell yourself / you may sugarcoat yourself.

To swallow the thing you have become: the sun, or a half-sunken sculpture.

Of Apollo's chariot rising from a pond in crumbling Versailles, the dry.

Eye of its drowning horse transmitting *see me, see me*—

As if the stampede.

To live depended on the existence of a witness, the empathetic presence.

Of a candysucking audience: *If a stone beast falls in the water, and no one.*

Watches her shatter—

II

Perfect month of spring: a woman in the garden.

Twirling her umbrella, clothed in tulle confections.

Propped in the environment, not reacting to it. She is the one creating this universe.

II

        I pulled as hard as I could, my back broke down.

By the weight of a dying master, by the incommunicable sadness of wings.

Never tested till the moment of disaster—

                   Apollo shouting *faster! Faster!*

III

Shhhh—the Beloved *is* here, surrounded by flowers.

A wave lifts her up, then dissolves into fairies.

Fairies lift the petals, and they become a fragrance bottle!

III

I used to be like you, and shone like you, and lived to make certain the sun.

Rose, like you.

IV

Don't disappear! Shine brighter.

Don't scatter in the breeze—collect yourself for tourist photographers.

Don't spill an inch outside your allotted body, green branches. It's springtime, you have work to do.

IV

Whip on the water: stop.

                    Blood on the plot.

                                      This devotion: a curse: nothing.

Seems worth saving.

V

The Beloved asks what I know about longing.

Enough, it seems, to drown myself in love.

Unanswered I become a grotesque relic, glorifying the garden with the uselessness of being.

V

To love is to drown
In a substance you once
Begged to consume you

I was born I was raised
I was built this way
To be the beast

Who carries her master
On her back like a prayer
A faith that makes light

Shine from previously
Dark spaces in case of
Emergency please beat

Me please whip me
Senseless so that I may
Transcend my bestial

Limitations and surface
From this crisis
Blessed and subservient

Pointed toward
The Palace and loving
Every minute of it

It may disgust you to discover such decadence.

Rejects progress. Wisteria, flamboyant, anticipates your life.

Captured as a picture by a man in Ushijima; hung upon a wall to conjure peace in times of strife.

I was born I was raised
I was built this way
A stone replica

Of my true self
Sculpted with Apollo
To abandon the east

And make the sun
Rise flamboyantly
From a mistaken

Direction the king
Sings *west* and money
Makes it so

In the Mercury
Drawing
Room the hour

Strikes daylight
On the Automaton
Clock and thus

Louis XIV and Fame
Appear, descending
From a cloud.

VI

Wartime Paris new millennium: *Merciful Clouds All Protecting*.

Scene number seven: wisteria, full flower, in front of a pavilion.

Tree peonies and flowering peaches blooming simultaneously.

VI

In Versailles, "The History of Fountains" is transmitted every evening

As *A Mythological Love Dream*, and again the next morning as *Propaganda*

The shocking story stars a beast built to drive our heroic Sun God

To the heavens in a glamorous gilded chariot to conjure dawn

And thus: *enlightenment*. I appear to the public: therefore I exist

A spectacle to titillate the aristocracy between visits to the boudoir

And teatime, wired to shine not for the gods but for their chic

And powdered patrons—I adore them for the way they pump

Enough water for the entire population of Paris into the pond

I am currently drowning in. May they be amazed, may they be

Overwhelmed by waterworks, by my crisis of faith, by the desire

To save me, and thus cause the day: now frozen: to break open

From the breeze the Beloved itself is beautiful when the blossom crawls across it there is nothing else.

From the Beloved the blossom itself is beautiful when the breeze crawls across it there is nothing else.

From the blossom the breeze itself is beautiful when the Beloved crawls across it there is nothing else.

VII

From the sky the earth itself is beautiful when the sun crawls across it there is nothing else

obsession

From the earth the sun itself is beautiful when the sky crawls across it there is nothing else

obsession

From the sun the sky itself is beautiful when the earth crawls across it there is nothing else

obsession

obsession

obsession

VIII

Afterwards, perhaps, permission to be beautiful will come directly from your captors.

For now the gloss of April remains your finest hour.

It's no secret, you know, the true nature of all creation.

VIII

Was grounded by the inadequacy you saw in me.

                                        Was grounded by the rush

and the how to

                of wings never seen

                                but strapped to my back like a master, a camera

without whose gaze

                the looked-at would cease to exist—

                                                you see, I was built

to do this.

                A beast carved of stone to carry you.

                                        Whip dancing down, sun

stuck in its watery rut.

                My faith: a weight

                                I chose to disclaim, so that I might

be *light* enough to fly again—

                        I asked, and I heard nothing.

                                                I believed that I

was dying.

                Yet all along we were rising out of the water,

                                        not falling into it,

and when I finally saw myself

                from a distance,

                                through the sugarsoaked

The ultimate ownership: *to make sense out of you.* I've got a perfect way.

To be the Patriarch in a garden, in all my grim beauty: one bare breast, nursing.

Our infant child, a duplicated image that illuminates my monstrosity.

eyes of a candysucking audience,

Apollo was soaring—

and it was the existence

of a witness that carried him.

The way things actually grow invites metaphor.

Petals spread across the grass, an icy path; loops of racemes in a honeycomb pattern.

Matter so familiar, the world we walk through becomes strange.

TRUTH TO MATERIALS

From the microphone of one headset to the earpiece of another: descriptions
Of the village in winter, a remembrance of your mother, news of the revolution
Over post office paint color—ambition, desire, the allure of glittery water,
Fantasy, torture, cinematic corpses. Your typical conversation. A question. Blank
Waiting. The question asked again; a hum; coughing; and then the words get said
That will never be forgotten: *a horrible explosion* or "I think she's still in love
With him," whatever, it doesn't matter: drunk gossip, static chatter—but outside
Of your window, the city starts to fissure, *a projection of your body*: a building,
A lobby, a high-rise turned to rubble (your heartbeat as it stumbles), dust clouds,
Some crying, stories of denial, anger, now cursing, and then you start
Rebuilding: a gleaming glass metropolis, transparent, believable, a corridor of
Crystal, enlightened, methodical, a vulnerable construction, true to its materials.
The will of a person translated into space may result in an edifice architected
To reflect the world not as it appears, but as it was once dreamed to be: honest.
Knowable. Twinkling gold with certainty. A see-through bridge, an illuminated
Tower, *a faceted glass skin that unfolds like a crystal flower*—where nothing is hidden;
Yet everything is permitted; and in that gleaming new utopia I would be gifted
With clairvoyance, and the ability to stare into structures whose windows once
Reflected only atmosphere, cloud cover, fickle weather. A city is made for
Falling. A veil drops only because it was born to reveal you. I could not awaken
To the conversation's bleak revelation, and so I begged the headset to transmit
The truth to me, turn the city to glass for me, that the world might be naked
And shimmering, *shivering*, and I could see through to the hearts of buildings.

LA MAISON DE LA PUBLICITÉ

Chews off branch / abandons bloom in trap.
Heart fills with so much love nothing can contain it.
Bust out of one box / get caught in another.

LA MAISON DE LA PUBLICITÉ

Under the auspices of solar genesis, we awoke in the New Year to discover the city was still there. Can you fathom that disappointment? Oh, love would find a way to save us from divine annihilation, even if we begged it not to. I spoke to you through your messagebox and the mutual friend who appeared from the east and dying on our doorstep, drinking himself to *make the dream look real again*, revolve the end-of-things to face the fresh millennium, again. "You cannot go back," the masses thought together, "you must go forward" floated the slogan like a suggestion above the world's collective head. Below such signposts we were filled with dread and chilled the champagne in the coldbox, and kissed nervously, and fastened streamers of gold and green to the high Victorian ceiling, which was busy standing in for the sky. That's when our friend, carrying his body and barely standing, arrived. We call a person "obliterated" but what we really mean is *an ungraspable force is standing in for him*, a policy of symbols has exiled his value system to a lost delirium, again. Think of last century's *Media Wall*. Think of a structure built to be covered by a changing array of illuminated signs—sentimental, commercial, antagonistic (by design), shifting, *transmitting*, to feed you and your distraction machine. Back to our friend's appearance at the requisite feverish party scene. This "End of Things" was an evening enabled by the progress of public consciousness, by the evolution of our species toward wearing glittery cardboard celebration hats while stockpiling against urban terrorism. It was Times Square all over again—a police army helicoptered in to protect a carnival; a kiss at midnight to portray Time and Desire, and the sexy way they both love and murder one another. Under the kitchen cupboard, partiers anxiously iced a chocolate cakebox that would soon stand in for everything they ever wanted, but had not yet tasted when our friend called from the phonebox inside the parkbox and said "I have driven here from Phoenix to testify I'm already dead—and so, you cannot save me. Pray for me. This year is killing me. *It kills me when you breathe with me.*" Hang up the phone, dear. Drop the cherries on the cake. And do not, I repeat *do not* answer the door. That is what the messagebox is for. That is why we invented *rewind* and *review* and *delay*, to stutter the entrance of the inevitable, to enable instant replay. To witness in slow motion, an acceleration toward dying, leaves a person powerless, yet captivated, by another's suffering. What can you offer that is worth offering? When he finally arrived on our doorstep, we embraced him and pretended his message had never

The modern pergola, clad in mirror-glass. Facing a second:

Purplish toward the calyx. Standing between structures, a tourist is uncertain—

Are these hanging reams of racemes reflections, or the real thing?

existed—*speak of it and the façade will fall*—think of last century's *Media Wall*. Beaming a surface from his body so liquid it was possible we would drown in him, *believe in him,* where was the friend I'd lost again, spinning faster than most planets at the end of the millennium—again. Billboards on his building broadcast "The body has quit but the mouth keeps drinking—" So Hopkins became our current thinking: *The glassy peartree leaves and blooms,* our friend, the Phoenix, had risen too soon—the countdown to New Year's had not yet begun, but there he expired, having fun, blowing his noisemaker, licking his party favor, while our guests sat glued to the television. *The invented logic of dreams* . . . the body performing in space . . . Ziggy Stardust, The Thin White Duke, Aladdin Sane . . . in the dream we held him . . . and bathed him . . . and were saved by him . . . again. . . .

TULLE

Early summer flowers.
Differing a little in color.
From those of the main spring blossoming.

TULLE

Game in which every building you enter stands in for an experience you cannot remember.

May: you enter the abandoned structure: hopes for the future scattered like paper.

Flowers across the Badestrand, carousing till the second cock, dressed in love and a hundred.

Dollar house frock. Wandering through the game Palace—hey, these mirrors aren't old.

They've been "distressed," what you're meant to *feel* here is anybody's guess: learning to lose.

Your way again. You've returned to the same damn building again. To change the rules.

Of its architecture: *the spring betrayal never happened here:* MC Memory and his indefatigable.

Turntable spinning you into the revision factory. Game in which every minute you spent.

On the Beloved becomes a room that you must live through: keep in mind the torture view.

Available from every balcony, hopes for the future cast down, yesterday's wilted desire—

Wisteria strangling the cable wire. At the very moment we grasp an image, the image turns.

And changes (attempt to translate your previous love by scanning the Palace pages).

Summer before the inevitable fall: a kiss stolen between the blueprint and the wrecking ball.

Game in which the way out of your Palace is to remember a star-crossed transaction.

Exactly as it happened: forget the mirrors, they're only distractions: and please put the balcony.

Behind you. Only the present can save you. The turntable is looping "The End of Things" again—

You've forgotten the rules of the game again? The past and the present cannot both be real.

At the same time, silver bells ring their revelatory chime: only you can see the game Palace.

You're stuck inside—ah, sweet trap, it has you hypnotized, imprisoned by rapturous dreams.

Of a fake yet perfect empire, lost and withered wisteria still killing the beloved cable wire.

BEAUTY. TRUTH. TENDERNESS.

Aging vine trained through a trellis.
Each drooping head hung through a square.
Writhing over a shallow pool, that you may be mirror'd the better.

BEAUTY. TRUTH. TENDERNESS.

And on that evening the very things you had tried to hold up came crashing.

Down upon you, careening, yet shining, *a tumbling rosevine* or *principles for falling*.

In love with your enemies at the start of this century and who knew it would be.

The one you loved the most who would turn around and fuck you? The archetype.

For this painful scenario was whipped up a long long time ago. Baby, they do it.

Because they can, cooed the aging rockstar to the lipglossed teenfan, biting.

Down bitterly his candied erection. In the cool labyrinth of revenge we lose.

Our direction: to uphold these same truths we rest on. The last time I saw you.

You had that Jupiter smile on. Boundary of the gods, they say, properly called.

Intellectual, Plato's dynamic planet, charming light from the dullest black hole.

It was no wonder we longed to be near you, as your *presence* shoved us straight.

From the skyframe (Yo, Allah: top of the celestial food chain). To explain.

How December had now overcome her, the exile said to the translator: *Because.*

I have lost the way to my city, my city forever will haunt me. Like a first kiss beneath.

The cherry tree? *Not exactly.* Or a lonely night dreaming of treasure ships?

That's more like it. Pleasure is immediate, words are the clothes of ideas and thus.

To truly *feel* the meaning of a statement it is essential that first you undress it.

Ah—the booty inside the sunken ship! Let us then, to the best of our ability.

Sweet Enemy, celebrate this festival of "bad energy" and general not-getting.

Alongness, which my lost self renders illustrious by its sacrifices of dignity.

And loyalty to those who screw me—Jupiter is both shadowing and shining.

Upon thee. This candyass labyrinth you are lost in is the earthly stage.

We stand on—the curtain of your Riot Act has fallen. Love, I will play the hand.

I am dealt. May the rose vine unpetal its meaning; may the audience discover itself.

CONSTRUCTION OF AN ARTIFICIAL WORLD THAT REPLACES OUR BODIES WITH AN INTRICATE ASSEMBLY

Does this endless longing convince you.

Aromatic flowers bloom magnificently underwater.

And the idyllic world beyond what you call *paradise* is actually within reach?

CONSTRUCTION OF AN ARTIFICIAL WORLD THAT
REPLACES OUR BODIES WITH AN INTRICATE ASSEMBLY

Request not the dismantled Amber Room, it has been stolen from you, it is lying hidden.

Inside a damp mine or beneath the spellbound sea, while the Beloved lies indigo sleeping.

Does the Beloved dream of me? Be vigilant in your intellectual part, warned the translator.

For sleep about this has an infinity with real death, and I listened then, and I considered.

The heart, how it can be held in another's hands, while the mind remains a lost chamber.

Unfolding in mirrors, escaping—nothing, and everything. Whomsoever has been lost.

To another, know that "lose" is derived from the thought portraying "untying," to split.

A piece of wood in half is to feel the original tree felled long ago while inside.

Your mind that tree is fast expanding—multiplying—I have been here before.

Trembling beneath the black and melting cube of sleep, the cold embrace of sweet.

And wrecked insomnia, before the predicted flight of the original Beloved, before echoes.

Of an Amber Room, its ambrosial tune tempting my lovelorn craftsman to *put it back.*

Together again, before the translator had written, in sand, of the inevitable split between.

My alleged heart / my alleged head, before the word evolved from what was meant.

To what is said, there is where I wish to live. Preserved inside a masterpiece of glowing.

Amber. Be persuaded that those things are not your riches that you do not possess.

Including the prophecy portraying "thinking," the way by which I fathom another asleep.

As I, awake, lie crying, understand that no dissimulation can be long concealed.

What you "know" is what you "feel," make trial of those who would teach you otherwise.

Now, close my eyes. Take me back to sleep with you. I fear I've found the Amber Room.

I fear you've found another.

Your mother wove vines to make your jacket, trousers, stockings, and shoes.

She also made a bow and arrow.

When you step into sun, you will explode into blossom.

COPPEROPOLIS

Intense bursts of energy are now emanating from the sun. And you are lit from within.
Like it ain't no thing. "I am lit from within!" The seconds so facile to glitter through.
But there is only so much a light switch can do for you. Soon the fog resolves the gold.
Situation into a more recognizable Gray Area, a wet terror turning luscious; a tropical.
Hysteria. Queen Suburbia, you have the inalienable right to be both depressingly awful.
And insanely beautiful, simultaneously. They say that to illuminate the unknown way.
You must embody a perfected degradation, until your true core resembles a collection.
Of luxe yet outdated cartophilia. To revivify your spent imagery: reflect a subdivision.
Beneath the consolidated sun, speak in tongues of a wrecked grandeur, build a private.
Architecture of Elizabeth Taylor, a screaming Judy Garland solar system, wear despair.
As if it were a Renzo Pianoed, couture cage—oh careful, dear, of what you weigh, lest.
You burst the bars of this edifice. (There was a time I could not have imagined this.
Before the unearthing of my lost Copperopolis.) Every breathing body has a city buried.
Beneath the surface of its false yet certain shimmer—Zut! *You drink yourself insensitive.*
You kill the morning with a jailbait hangover, and when your outside aches as much.
As your interior's hidden sadness, you cry until your vanquished metropolis shines . . .
And lo! You are lit up from the inside! A Jules Verne spaceship that cannot fly—

Swamp Bayou Two o'Clock. Louisiana climber Pondside Blue.

U.S. wisterias more hearty, less invasive than the Asian species.

Stop dazzling! Be unspectacular. Stay exactly where you're supposed to be.

TO SLEEP IN FAME

Of the time when you knew nothing and therefore everything: nineteen and hurtling toward a smashing.

Sea on your tricked-out motorcycle, the melting English countryside at turns insouciant then obsessed by.

Your fever dream: to be at the center of history: to burn forever in a bonfire glamour: untouched by death.

Unbroken by landscape, flying both into and over the road like a—soul?—floating above the body, stunned.

And newly uncertain of its relation to the—person?—it has chosen to inhabit, a hideous and often didactic.

"Body of Evidence" within this image workspace (behind the poem's dense clockface I can almost *feel* you.

Praying I'll stop pinching your nipples for this voyeuristic camera——) here is the beloved character.

Portrayed as Ambition within a stanza, here is an abstraction of Fame as "the mechanical form we ride on."

Ah! the obvious autofetish! the author's imperial advantage! the young man suspended like a thought above.

A thinking he soon will inhabit: racing through the moment: as if brave acceleration could save him: hurtling.

Toward a smashing sea with the intensity of fever dreams: the drive toward death killing the dull tick of time.

(And with this view of autonomy in mind: it is the saddest thing in the world that I came along to haunt you.)

Little messages of all colors, attached to great racemes in the courtyard of a temple.

May the briskness of your growth.

Be a good omen for our future marriage.

THE ENGAGEMENT

In Rome a shrink-wrapped bust of Nicollò Machiavelli.

In Rome our story of love, swaddled in petroleum jelly.

In Rome a wide-screen Pope restored the holy square.

In Rome a whorish kiss beside a relic gate-to-nowhere.

In Rome The Cure of Autonomy was an illusory condition.

In Rome I wept inside the ring, a virgin blushed by Titian.

In Rome A System of Togetherness rewired my frontal lobe.

In Rome *all that matters are my feelings and my wardrobe.*

In Rome de Chirico's paintbrush, tarted up for millennium hoards.

In Rome a hypodermic needle—our restored and glistening sword!

In Rome I touched a ruin near hosed-down stone arcades.

In Rome we fought and then embraced *a bubblegum charade.*

In Rome my self eroded within our union's holy writ.

In Rome a kitchy allegiance to the preservation of our—

In Rome a diamond ring passed over time and cappuccino.

In Rome a gambler's bluff unveiled by Truth in the Casino.

In Rome our map did not hold true, the city divided by time.

In Rome the white-hot rock transformed Free Will into a crime.

In Rome I begged the question: can one survive when caught?

In Rome this voice was not for rent (in Rome this voice was bought).

In Rome Jubilee Gates unlocked, a beggar's hand unfurled—

In Rome in love *in form* I stood newly ruined at the center of the world.

You could pose in front of the wisteria holding a vine away from your body like a prize fish.

You could tie a wish to its trunk with a wide satin ribbon.

You could pour a cup of sake, then empty some on the tree's roots in hopes of contributing to its great size, and beauty.

MAKING HISTORY

Did you do it.
Consciously? Cherry.
Blossom set to.
Automatic spring.

Trained to grow around the house.

Clusters 8 inches; seductive fragrance; 13 leaflets; flower standard whitish; wings and keel, sea lavender violet.

Despite appearances: may be a hybrid.

ORNAMENT AND CRIME

A horse with a golden horn glued to its head; a centaur stuck between.
Surrealism and uselessness; a pack pony strapped to a jewel-encrusted.
Tent; oh how these years without you have fashioned me into a parody.
Of ornamentation and its discontents! The future as you remember it.
Does not include a version of my body covered in scrims of decoration.
Or silver-studded clouds hanging over my expertly lacquered head—
Maybe you were expecting a shivering, transparent girl instead? Layer.
Upon layer of meretricious exteriors are required to uncover The Real.
Distorted by smoother surfaces that invite consumption. So stick it.
Where the sun don't shine. Perhaps you'll find the pulchritude of such.
Mutations kind of just sneaks up on you, as a mirage of candied colors.
And floating palm trees leads to the desert's deep dysfunctions. Huh?
Honesty is always the best policy. I am so "not over it." The future I.
Once chose has become more real than the future I was given: thus.
My beloved artifice falls beneath a critique of purest reason. Can't.
You see what you have done? Time to put my utopic, equestrian skin.
Back on. A dying field of fennel rolls and bucks as I walk through it.
Sparrows flit from limb to limb in chaotic diagrams of how we come.
To lose a home. My braided mane stuck with flowers; a golden rope.
Tied to my neck. Visit me like a ruin. Demolish me with tenderness.

A MICROCOSMIC SOCIETY WHICH SETS AN EXAMPLE TO THE REST OF AMERICA AS TO HOW ONE SHOULD BEHAVE IN LARGE GATHERINGS

These "Oriental" specimens upon which you base your descriptions.

Expired in the heat of a Surrey peach house . . . midsummer, getting older.

Easy to ripen. Harder to bloom.

A MICROCOSMIC SOCIETY WHICH SETS AN EXAMPLE TO THE REST OF AMERICA AS TO HOW ONE SHOULD BEHAVE IN LARGE GATHERINGS

If a carver sees the future in a hunk of uncut jade, which is more real, the sculpture.

Or the stone that's carved away? In the beginning was a love affair that ended badly.

And in the end were remains to be grasped, like ashes, billowing out of our hands.

Whosoever struts as a peacock struts across a stadium rock stage may be blinded.

By the minions swirling in sweating flurries—to music!—within the mosh-pit bowl.

Below (memo to Mick: a spotlight shone on a body don't infuse the body with soul).

Consider The Individual, a tightly corseted continuum of light and ashes contained.

Just barely within a structure aching to diffuse its diaphanous heart in a burst of self.

Revelation: an exodus we call "falling in love" or "abandoning one's proper station."

And spilled myself all over the place. Because I could not be the songbird I found.

Another to croon my favorite tune; thus it was with unrivaled relief I let myself.

Pour into you, releasing rays of light to spitshine the microphone. Get yer ya-ya's.

Out? No, Altamont ain't what this poem is about, angels patrolling the sidelines.

With pool cues, the empty beer can cum popular weapon, Keith Richards eyeing.

A "bad situation" under the powertrip thumb of a popshow singalong. My love.

Hindsight won't right what has been wronged; pack up the show, put your pimp.

Cloak on; abandon the stage where your minions have wept; this leonine moment.

Is as good as it gets. The map for finding home unfolded timely as a flower, yet.

Alone on my dark road I could not let go the shards of light, the ash, the hour—

Number of branches 9,000, flowers 675,000.
5 petals, 10 stamens; 7 ovules for 4 million seeds; in the anthers, if perfect: 27 billion grains of pollen brought by bees.
Such petals placed end to end would extend the distance between us, or *34 miles*.

HEADSET

The sun gives us our genesis, he said, but is not itself the genesis of our being. Connected.
Yet portable, I countered, sauntering down the carpeted hallway speaking seductively into.
My floating microphone. Much like the current rash of popshow singers, who may dance.
As if possessed by demons while lipsynching, who breathe into their cordless conduits.
Coupled, yet unattached. A goal being to have one's cake and eat it, too, to ramble over.
Earth alone while still transmitting thoughts and feelings to whoever may be listening.
The sun has brought us into existence, he whispered furiously, but is not the same thing.
As existence, it makes us visible, and yet—he was not jacked into his headset. Clutching.
His handset as though grasping for my faraway shoulder, but my limbs were free then.
And I poured yesterday's murky flower water into the sink. I see, I said, you have loved.
Then lost the Beloved. It is your fault, he growled, you forced me to say what I think.
His voice fell into my earpiece, a dreamer awakening from sleep. Plugged in yet utterly.
Unhinged. Years ago the drowsy child was told that as she slept her soul would drift.
High above her body, and as it wandered they would be tethered by an invisible cord.
Of light. And if the cord breaks? What then? Ring ring. Time to be yourself again.

INTERPRETING THE MOOD OF THE WORLD AND TURNING IT INTO THINGS THAT PEOPLE WANT

If petals were pages you could scan me *full bloom*.
"But the flowers fall faster than I can read them!"
Under the tree, grasping at light, empty in the fertile season.

INTERPRETING THE MOOD OF THE WORLD AND
TURNING IT INTO THINGS THAT PEOPLE WANT

A winter solstice spent sitting cross-legged on a couch with the volume turned down.

Low, lethargic from tranquilizers and tumblers of Coca-Cola; depicted in a gardener's.

Textbook as *a fragile houseplant*, and after the narcotics kick in as *a vase filled to the brim*.

With Casablanca lilies. It was meant to open like a lily inside me, a bud both earthy.

And somehow cosmic, alone yet flirting with the infinite, the way a single flower.

May correspond to a celestial body by mimicking its more desirable properties.

Such as beauty visible from a long distance, a sparkly chimerical flatness, a sinful.

Petal system over a heavenly virginal face (bare bottoms peeking out through.

Ivory lace)—Oh Yves Saint Laurent, is it time for my next dose of controlled.

Euphoria? Twelve days post-miscarriage, sprawled atop a chaise longue reading.

Of your penchant for shoulder pads, of your pathological fear that all you adore.

Will be replaced when you're not looking, the Mondrian dresses, *le smoking*.

The safari look, the military styles, the *chouette* Moroccan houseboy and perfectly.

Ordered vials. Such a refusal to accept life's customary regrets could be diagnosed.

As melancholy, as manic inability to let the past . . . abandon you . . . as sex drive.

For facsimile, a falsified geography, an allegiance to the feeling that nothing slips.

Away from you, sprawled atop a stainless steel table, watching the doctor point.

Inaudible soundwaves at a perfect angle. A new star was scheduled to appear.

On the silver screen, but silence was detected where a heart should have been.

"Yves has never seen a Gucci dress," his lover said. "It doesn't exist for him."

Fortune was shown a beautiful specimen.

Flourishing in a ruined garden on an island near Xiamen.

Kissing violet blooms, hacking roots with an axe, restoring balance the following season.

PARADISE CITY

You know, babe, like when you met me at the shickey-shack island airport
In your *Aloha* car, and with my tootcase in your backseat we extravagated
Betwixt uninterrupted palm trees that announced the road as being
A controllable narrative, itinerant clouds collecting as mythically scripted
To warn the community of corrupt social policy or the serial killer hiding
Behind recently renovated sand dunes, the machete-wielding rickety-rick
From a closed down sugar-cane factory who no one will tell the tourists
About, lest they sashay their pup tents to the Jurassic Park of yo purty island's
North Shore, which is smack dab where we ended just two poondays later
On what alleged to be a jaunt to the rain forests yet coyly revealed itself
As an emergency beeline to your yurt-dwelling drug dealer, I was clueless
With my point-and-click, trolling the cliff side for toucans and movie
Stars, it's outstanding the way you foiled me, I should really take a lesson
In your brand of "transportation," in the pineapple mechanics of *haole*
Engineering, then I can be a strung-out deceptor, a sexy thwarter of island
Order, I'll goofily resystematize the clockwork of this ticking tiki paradise—
What else, really, is there to do? Scour beaches for rickety-rick? Suck decaying
Sugar cane? Turn your *Aloha* around, and take me back to the you know.

BRIDAL

Last flower of spring.
Unable to release itself and attain perfection.
Gorgeous pale brocade, arms reaching earthward!

BRIDAL

The translator approaches the box and the box begins its story. "Not long.
After the Italian engagement I was built to contain her hopes, her dreams.
Her worries. Every season has a notebook of fashionably sexual perversions.
—June adores her ladies, but seems to have outgrown foreplay, hipcocked.
In the hallway exhibiting perfect politesse, wrapped up inside her diamond.
Ring and a black-lace babydoll dress (*Marriage and Insanity:* the ultimate.
Feminist text). Stretched taut upon the clothesline of domestic marital.
Bliss, she wrote her vows, concealed her flaws, and sealed June with a kiss.
Late at night long after her intended fell asleep, she opened my lid, shoved.
A tongue in my ear, and wooed me with her secrets. Lipstick cherry all over.
Corseted tortoise in finery: mutton dressed as lamb? (Make sure you wear it.
With irony.) Shoving her manicured finger down a ripped and frilly nightie.
Dropping *les petit soins* like an autodidact kinderwhore. She exhibited *maybe* two.
Of the qualities a heroine must possess: talent, beauty, and a tragic lack of cash."
Note: I was never that girl. I was that boy. I'm not that person at this point.

THE BUTTERFLY ROOM

Thousands of metallic racemes.
Cascading from the teahouse trellis: I arrange myself beneath the blossoms' shade.
And disappear into deep purple.

THE BUTTERFLY ROOM

Cocooned, predictably: the walls glazed and sealed to look like candy. Tasty.

Hey baby—what's up with lifting the drapes of my heart with water drops.

And restrained agony, what's up with these wings growing on the wrong side.

Of my body, you're teetering in a caftan as you slink into your genie bottle—

Archon of a penthouse filled with *objets* that cannot harm you, organic gold.

Tomatoes, Marilyn's *blanco* piano, constructing yourself from energy trapped.

Inside me / underwater—devotional domestic space never seemed so. . . .

Dreamlover. When the world outside stops threatening you with Modernism.

And Richard Serra, you'll untwine your umbilical tiara to let this womb.

Abandon you—

And then when I am empty and the child sits beside me, I'll rub my belly in wonder.

To wonder—if I have been destroyed from the inside by beauty, if I am what spring.

Has left behind. Let no man question this perfect sadness, lest he grow wings, and fly.